new writing from the west
Alan Hayes, Nuala Ní Chonchúir, Editors

Órfhlaith Foyle

Revenge

To my family

Revenge

Órfhlaith Foyle

First published by Arlen House in September 2005

Arlen House
PO Box 222
Galway
Ireland
Phone/fax 086 8207617
arlenhouse@ireland.com

ISBN 1-903631-74-2, paperback
ISBN 1-903631-94-7, signed and numbered limited edition

Typesetting: Arlen House
Printed by: ColourBooks, Baldoyle, Dublin 13
Cover image is of an 'Ethiopian Cross' from the author's collection

Contents

ACKNOWLEDGEMENTS

A selection of Órfhlaith Foyle's poems and short fiction have been published in *The Stinging Fly*, *The Shop* and *Galway Now*. Her critically acclaimed short story, 'Sweet Frankie', is published in the new Arlen House anthology, *DIVAS! A Sense of Place*, edited by Nuala Ní Chonchúir.

My thanks are due to Nuala Ní Chonchúir and Alan Hayes for their advice and encouragement.

Photograph of Her Brother's Skull - Serbia

They give you to me,
A numbered skull from a high shelf
And in my hand you are
A strange brute thing - a thing I hardly see -
My brother.

The clean smooth bone of you -
The whole of you no longer with me.
In this room of discovered skulls,
I have lost my memories
And the photographer fixes your dead stare
For his lens.

In this room of skulls,
Your face is lost,
My brother,
And I grip hard to what is left.

There Is A Painting I Know

There is a painting I know
With a mad, slithering light.
And it succours every crazed eye.
In it
Desperate lovers
Kiss.
Isolated drinkers
Drink.
And the painter,
- His lips to my shoulder -
Says merely
'This is a slice of Damnation'.

Damn Them

Damn the purists
And their love of rightness.
Their pure fear of love.

Give me life.
Give me Gods.
Give me flesh.

Damn pristine elite-ness
Of manner,
Cool, well-toned voices
Cautious and serene.
Damn manufactured spirits
Of beauty
Of careful love
Of controlled lives.

Give me wide, wild spirits.
Give me terrible, tumbling passion
Give me love
That rips my soul
Open to you.
Give me the lust of your eyes
That slams against my body.
Give me your wetness,
Your skin.

I damn their hateful saintliness,
Their rules of normality.
They watch us with snake-like caution.

We love
You and I
And Damn Them.

Bush Wife

Once she was reduced to begging.
Slipping to her knees, her mouth
At his ear.
'This is your conscience speaking'.
And she magicked a desperate smile.
'Bring me back something sweet,
Something kind,
Or chocolate'.
But he left as usual,
Thirty miles into the Bush towards town,
Thought of her only as the remnant,
Something to pick up when he got back.
Pick up and twist when
She was useful again.
'By the way', he mentioned once,
'Three men died in the hole we dug today'.
He looked at her as he ate:
'Funny. Life is cheap here'.

These Things Exhilarate My Soul

These things exhilarate my soul:
Bark underfoot.
A vast wind's terrible brilliance.
An uncurled sun at night.
And you. Just you.

The Stranger

To grow in one place.
To root your feet and say
'I am of this place.
The skin of this people's skin is mine.
Their talk, my talk.
Their smell is mine'.
You prefer the stranger to remain lost.
His talk could unleash witches' spells
So you don't listen to his story.
Yet you watch his skin and in pubs,
In houses like your own,
You talk about the stranger,
Relieved he is not you.

Despite Everything

Despite everything.
Despite it all.
This comes …
With the late day's
Evening breath.
Where are you to feel all this?

After Sunday Mass in Malawi

After Sunday Mass they whispered:
'He was a poet, perhaps.
A dissident, yes.
He ignored the spies in his classroom'.
Then someone else also remembered:
'Of course, this is not our country.
We are Whites, you see
And cannot disappear so easily'.

Missed Opportunity

One evening I walked
With someone I nearly knew.
He spoke of Alaska and cabin fever,
Trees in Ashland, Oregon
LSD and apparitions of
God.
Of course I was already in love
With someone else,
Not too different
And reasonably safe.

Dance

Imagine me in a man's arms
The buttons of my dress pressed into his shirt.
Music and evening sun
The kind of heat that gives sheen to everyone's skin.
I taste my man's sweat as I kiss his chest where
His shirt is unbuttoned to his breast-bone.
I lay my forehead where I've kissed him.
I can smell us both.
Feel his lips in my hair.
This life.
This need to seep into and love not only him
But what is around us.
The laughing, drunk sixty-year-old woman in the corner,
Low slung orange dress and puckered breast,
Red lips reciting poetry she composed yesterday to a young male
A student of her life.
He wants her thirst for life.
My lover holds my waist.
Our hip-bones find anchor in each other.
Old men's eyes gleam.
They smoke cigars and drink local brandy.
They watch us dance and sing.
Their own voices add to the slow gut-drive of a lone trumpet.
It's good to be who I am
In my lover's arms.
I think of our bed and the stone floor.
Shutters - never curtains.
The bristling, hot human night outside.
My love, I call him.
My love.

And Where Else?

Sometimes we were mistaken for Canadians
And because we replied Australian,
We seemed to make sense.
School friends demanded why we weren't black
Since we came from Africa too.
And where else?
Well, we climbed ant-hills on the way to Mombasa.
Spoke Swahili but lived on Kikuyu land.
We avoided the secret police in Malawi,
Grew used to the prison fence that hid
'The Disappeared'.
And in Australia, we learned
Irish are preferred to English,
Greeks and Italians are nicknamed 'Wogs'
And Aboriginals must look good for tourists.
And where else?
There's Russia and Lenin's corpse,
Israel, bombs in the market place and
Turkish delight under our pillows.
And where else?
And it was easy to explain away.
Well ... you see, we'd say
Our parents are Irish
But really,
We're from somewhere else.

ITALIAN NUNS

In Kenya, we knew Italian nuns
Who snapped chicken necks
And swung pig sausage from the
Kitchen rafters.
They smelled of soup and incense
And dug their fingers into our cheeks -
A sign of endearment.
Dangerous women, we decided
And loved them back.
We dragged dead pigeons to their door
And walked barefoot in their rooms.
Sometimes they seemed to pray,
But when they called to the chickens,
My sister, brother and I
Sat, watched and waited.

If I Could

If I could
I'd pray for your resurrection
After four years
When I screamed inside
And remembered I must have loved you.
Instead, I am faced with other things:
The last drunken night and
That other body that smelled
Too sour and too real.

Religious Thoughts

Is God all love? All force. Life force.
Is love a force? We are loved
And fed well with this force,
Yet if we distil it, use it
For convenience,
May it not be evil?
And if so, if we cause evil
May it not reverberate against us?
So God ... loves us. Is us.
But if we misuse
Does not our love pervert us?

My words cannot delineate you
As Modigliani drew
From the dark Paris mornings
And later during the 'Terror'
You wandered mad at
The edge.
Three lovers gone.
A son imprisoned.
Perhaps the death-choked
Eyes of Tstvetayeva
Haunted you.
Beloved exiles beckoned.
But you,
You turned your body,
Tall, inviolate
And breathed
Blood-fingered air.

Revenge

You had forgotten my
Wolf-like tendencies.
Once your laugh had
Shamed my anxious lips.
I amused your eyes.
My love was nothing.

So I made you shiver.
I told you how
I longed to purge you
Of what you truly
Loved -
An appreciation of revered
Tackiness.
The sort you see on
Popular catwalks.

I reminded you.
Your hands skittered
At your breast.
I dredged up passionate words.
Your eyes stopped on my face.
My words smothered your little
Mundane heart.
Squeaked it clean.
I pleasured my soul.
I watched you dwindle.

Someone should have
warned you what
Love can do.

Quince Flowers

Quince flowers weave the daffodils into their spell.
Speak to her, they order.
Remind her of her future.
The earth has -

It has sucked on the
Woman's fleshed bones.
It has implored the wind to call her.
The wind curls at her ears,
Swoons at her throat.
It lies against her trembling
Heart - sodden with a
Terrifying promise.

'Allow me to end your life.
I will bleach your soul empty.
I will adorn you with bird song'.
Earth's blood will crawl your
Veins open to her kiss.
Death - a knowing beauty - will
Press your dying lips.
Her breath will rot you of educated fantasies.
They litter at your feet.
Do not touch!
Grant me your demise.
I shall melt your flesh.
Dance your disassembled bones anew
Into a new breathing.

The woman reaching
Allows the quince to
Bracelet her wrist.

The Daemon

You come alive as I rest.
To ponder my careful guidelines.
You rise shining from me.
You are lean.
Stalking my normal air.
You want my life riddled with you.
My eyes to speak of your demon beauty.
My hands to shape your desires.
You glide derisively within my learned beliefs.
You snarl at my timidity.
So ...
You enter my dreams.
Your eyes fill mine.
I breathe you hard.
I feel your smile curve.
I feel you.
But ...
When I am awake, you are gone - repelled.
Sliding into the seams of my skin,
To prowl in my hidden heart.
I keep you there.
Veiled.
Breathing only through my pen.

Later in Leningrad

There were no *troikas* that winter.
The Neva flowed and I had loved
No poets yet.
Instead I admired the preserved face of Lenin
As we were supposed to.
And there was St Basil's -
Icons, gold and beauty.
In a hairdressers, we sipped coffee and bought
Roubles with US dollars.

There was Olga, tall and in love with our
Canadian friend.
For two nights she loved him
And I studied how she grasped him.
In tea-rooms by the Arbat,
I was mistaken for an English girl
By soldiers who sang opera and tried
To make me smile.
And later in Leningrad -
I stood still.

I stood still.
And I remembered its first name.

Lady Macbeth

Oh Lady,
You are full of death
And consigned to hell.
Love has torn you down
And your Lord has turned his face.
The night is waiting black
And the blood, red on your
Fingers will not wash.

When your brain ceased to
Skew madly,
At him
At his adoring lovers
At all lies.
When he no longer held your
Foot in his palm,
Then your fingers fed stone
With all the blazing of your heart.
Claudel,
Tell me.
Is madness worth it?

GOODBYE

It is day.
You are leaving.
Over coffee we bid
Goodbye to the lives
We've loved.
To our mad nights
And the precious fears
We've treasured.
Inevitable.
But I am human enough
To pray that your dreams
Are braided with echoes of me.

SOMEONE CREPT UP TO ME

Someone crept up to me
Knowledgeable and sweet, with
An eye for my sins.
They spoke of belief.
They spoke of love.
They kept me close and
Prepared me a Bible.
Open pages of logical verse.
Sin and counter-sin.
Of blood revenge and life
Reined in with rules
That deemed me lost yet
Branded me a recoverable
Whore.
Their army, I was assured, possessed
God's Heart.
Their war and their will had
His Mark.
But I spat out their goodness
Like spare vomit from my lungs.
I developed my own sure Blasphemy.
I prefer my love with its own mind.
I prefer my belief with its own heart.

I'VE DISCARDED MY OLD SKIN

I've discarded my old skin
At the sea
With other split-open shells,
Purple dead mussels
And slivers of fish bone.
My hips will fit different hands.
I am simple again.
Born with extra spit and
Finally useless to you.

Betrayal

You slammed love away into
The cold quarters of your heart.
It creaked.
You poured bile to deaden it.
I saw all this
I lamented without your permission.
You were loved.
You were betrayed.
You maintain that true betrayal
Comes from a lover.
Ignorant lie.
We all strip our souls for any kind
Of love and anyone can betray
With panache.

Van Gogh Visits

Van Gogh visits
My blue and yellow room.
At first, he looks like his
Shifting portrayals
Then smiles like his self-portrait could.
He draws the crows in the air.
He sits cross-legged from me,
Admiring my blue and yellow depths.
Sunflowers beam at us, dancing in my cheap poster.

I tell him I hear the crows caw.
He shrugs.
I write about his face and he watches.
He will not paint for me.
Not even for my walls.
He moves about on strong feet.
His clothes smell of sweat.
He likes what my pen paints.
He knows I want his passion.

Van Gogh sits on
My blue painted Russian chair,
By my yellow table and smiles at my hunger.

Marie considered ignoring the priest who would not move off her veranda.

'I've come to get you'. He insisted. 'We'll travel in the Landrover. An hour, give or take'. He squinted and slapped dead a fly on the veranda post.

'You have to go', he insisted.

'Will he survive?' Marie asked.

'He's waiting', replied the priest and then stuck his fingers into the carved figures of her new rosewood table. He sucked his teeth as he admired the smooth wood, curving his hand against its rim.

'Those Hausa fellows were around so', he said.

'Yes', she said.

'Like coming here, don't they?'

Marie rubbed her bare feet backward and forward on the veranda floor. She loathed Fr. Timothy. His large face and slit eyes always noticed things that sniffed of confession. She stood up and brushed her new, bright-flowered dress, then padded over to where she had left her sandals.

'That's good. That's good', said Fr. Timothy.

Marie half-rested against a veranda chair as she fastened each sandal. Her lungs hurt beneath the dress's bodice and she knew before evening came, it would be grimy with sweat. She used tissues from her handbag to pat her face dry as she walked across the small dirt compound to the waiting Landrover and sat in. She rolled down the window and wanted to cry.

The priest told the story. A bloody huge latrine and the boys in the sixth form class had been roped into digging along with her husband. Of course, he knew how to organise them. Got them their shovels, got them into a rhythm.

'They've songs for that', said Marie.

Fr. Timothy blinked. 'What?'

'They've their own methods', explained Marie. 'They don't need his'.

She was damned if she was going to play the role of loving wife. She licked sweat from her upper lip and inched her hips further away from Fr. Timothy's shadow on the seat beside her. She should have left before this. Forgot her husband, forgot the church, forgot Africa. Made her way to America to become one of those hippies. Long, long hair would have suited Marie.

'He loves his work', said Fr. Timothy, and continued with the story. A big, blasted hole, her husband at the bottom with two boys. Her husband climbed out and thought things were safe. Two minutes later, the hole collapsed and buried the boys. Fr Timothy looked at Marie.

'They couldn't be bothered to help us try and save them. Life is dirt-cheap here. But now they say it's all our fault. "Fucking white devils", they called us'.

Marie said nothing and gazed at the landscape. The hottest place next to hell, some well-meaning English ex-pat had told her at the club one night. He was a tall, gentle-faced man despite his heavy skin and drunk hands. Never mind, she thought, and allowed his hands pluck at the waistband of her skirt. She forgot his name soon enough. Forgot how he smelled when they half wrestled against an outside wall; forgot how she was supposed to play the game - just pretend it didn't happen. Add yourself to the rumour mill and if you perfect the colonial accent, you'll fit in just fine.

Her husband never listened to rumours. Instead he hit her. Once, even twice, she was prepared to forgive and she had the confession line down pat. Father, forgive me, I know everything I do. Somehow, even with that line, she could have wrangled forgiveness. You can wrangle almost anything, another lover told her once.

She remembered his hands most of all. Long, beautiful fingers held up towards a hotel room ceiling - and God, she loved what those fingers could do to her. She had fashioned a whole love from those fingers. They kept her alive, made her feel flesh and blood, and not just the punch-bag wife reflected in the bathroom mirror.

That lover wanted to save her and, most times, she was tempted to agree. Yes, I'll love you. I'll be the most glorious woman for you. I'll bring all my sin and beauty right to your door.

The fairy-tale never worked, but even with him gone she could still call up the image of his fingers onto her own and imagine how it could have been possible.

Marie steadied herself as the Landrover bumped its way into the police compound and drew up to the office headquarters. She got out and looked around for the baying mob, but there was nothing but the heat and the sound of laughter from the cook's kitchen.

Fr. Timothy lounged against the Landrover and jerked his head at the police commissioner's door. Marie patted at the creases in her skirt and went inside, smiled at the officer behind the desk and saw the shadow of her husband move behind the frosted glass of the commissioner's office. He and the commissioner were laughing. She sat on the low, brown bench and wished with all her heart that there was nothing left. Nothing of him. Nothing of her. Fr. Timothy came to the door and smiled.

'Soon get the pair of you back home', he said.

David heard the 'ssh ssh' of Fiona's deodorant spray and knew she was almost ready. She was supposed to be an actress and had acted in college. She acted still. She pounced on bit parts in the drama workshops that littered Galway. She had her dreams and she wanted her big break. Something to get her out of there, and she meant the actual shit of her life, although he had told her and made a compliment of it, that she was good at this, at him.

David was Galwegian and had no one to lie to. Fiona came from Cork, maybe had family roots, but chose Galway for its art life. She believed in God. 'I pray like a Russian', she mentioned when drunk. She believed in sex, in the life their bargain afforded her, and in her dream.

She also believed that David was like any other man. He liked games. He liked fucking and he enjoyed treats. All kinds of treats and, naturally, he paid more. Always that little bit more for that little bit extra. But he was bored now.

Instead, David found others on street corners or in pubs. Men and women whose bodies had an exciting, hard and grimy look. Bodies that fed that need in David, to be someone else, someone of substance and secrets.

Five years ago, Fiona had seemed like an answer. He had first seen her smoking outside the Town Hall during a play's intermission. When friends called her name, she waved them on, preferring to look at David. It was a look that nailed him. She walked up to him and said, 'I'm an actress. You?'

'Business man'.

'Enjoying the play?'

'Can't stand it'.

She smiled. 'It's supposed to be atmospheric, display inner conflict and have the promise of redemption'.

'Oh'.

They struck a bargain because she expected money and he liked the sight of her. Her body was thin and adaptable. Sometimes she seemed like a boy with a tight narrow walk and other times she spread like an earthy woman, hips wide; and she could laugh, hardly ever girlish, but sexy and promising everything.

David had never expected to grow used to Fiona. He had presumed her acting would guard against that, that she would continue to fascinate him with her characters, her voice, and, at times, he did attempt to wonder what was hers, absolutely hers, inside of her. There were moments when he played along and told her that he could lose himself inside her. Naturally she laughed. She held up her arms and said she was only skin; just skin to put on other people. 'On stage', she added.

David thought five years was a long time.

Fiona entered the room. She looked young. Her hair was blonde and fastened into curls. She wore a red pleated skirt with a narrow white blouse which she was unbuttoning. She glanced at David and re-did them. 'I'm tired', she announced.

David didn't respond.

Fiona sat on the carpet before his feet and fanned out her skirt across her thighs. A pair of old-fashioned spectacles peeped from her blouse pocket and her fingers were ink-stained. 'But I made an effort', she said.

'As what?'

'Semi-school girl. Lolita with brains'.

'I want something else', David said.

'I told you, I'm tired. Consider this the best you're going to get tonight. Give me another week and I'll think of something else'.

'You're not that good'.

'Christ, what a little prick you can be'. Fiona bent her head forward with a dramatic sigh, paused, then looked up again.

'Drink?'

'Fine', he said.

Fiona got to her feet and stretched to pluck an almost empty whiskey bottle from the fireplace mantelpiece. She held it under the room's light and shook it. 'It's cloudy', she remarked. 'Something must have got into it. Dust, probably'. She found two glasses and poured out their drinks and watched David as she drank. 'You're not touching yours'.

'Don't need it'.

Fiona poured more whiskey into her glass. 'I'm all ears', she said.

David looked at her. There were shadows under her eyes and a cold sore on her mouth, half-concealed by lipstick. 'I want to see you naked', he said.

Fiona shrugged. 'I usually am'.

'Just tonight, Fiona'.

She stared and said nothing. David lit a cigarette and watched her bare toes. Her nails had an old, yellow tinge and he felt an odd sickness in his gut, but he flicked ash onto the carpet and waited. Fiona stood up. She unbuttoned her blouse and dropped her skirt. She lifted one leg, then the other as she yanked off her underwear. Her blouse and spectacles fell to the floor. 'Look', she said.

He looked. He looked at a pale body going to fat at the shoulder blades and waist. He stubbed out his cigarette and for a long time said nothing.

Fiona put her clothes back on and sat beside him. She took a cigarette and lit it. She smoked and glanced at David before saying. 'I've a job. I must have forget to tell you'.

'Acting?'

'Yeah. In one of those old Irish plays Americans love. It'll do well in the festival. I'll be busy'.

'Getting your face known'.

'Yeah'.

David sat beside Fiona for a little while more. He supposed there was always some kind of ritual to a goodbye. Fiona drank her whiskey and he watched her. He said nothing and she said nothing, and, when he left her, she remained near the fireplace, looking at something else.

Everything about Jon was clean, whereas Susanne attracted dirt. It was in her nature. She loved summer for its hot, grubby moments and its people smell.

She never tired watching her own sweat gather like a second skin on her arms, and, in late afternoons, in her room and on her own, she'd lie naked on her bed, feeling her sweat cool into salt.

Susanne noticed Jon's feet when she and two friends decided to ditch work and spend the afternoon at the beach. Susanne wore her favourite swimsuit which was tight about her breasts; pressed them in so sometimes her breath caught and sparks flew in front of her eyes. She sat by a clump of stones, closed her eyes and pictured her bedroom where she could see herself lying on her bed, untying her swimsuit, peeling it down to her waist, sensing her sweat dry away and the heat of the room not quite warm enough to prevent her shiver.

'Excuse me', said a male voice.

Susanne opened her eyes and saw that a long, delicate foot had spread its toes on the stone above her shoulder, while its companion foot hung in the air. Water dripped from the body they were connected to. Susanne shielded her eyes and smiled upwards for two seconds, then looked back down at that pale foot. It had a large vein running from the ankle to its second toe. The toenails were pristine with white tips. She watched the foot flush pink just above its sole as it gripped the rock, while its companion landed onto a sandy patch.

'Do you mind?' said the owner.

'Not at all', said Susanne.

He had silky clean hair cut long over his ears and Susanne had no doubt if he pinned his hair back behind them, he'd look far too female. 'I'm Jon', he said and put out his hand.

She took it. 'Susanne'.

He nodded in the direction of sunbathers and sea-swimmers.

‘Always a surprise, isn’t it? The sun and an Irish summer. Maybe I notice it more because I’m not Irish’.

‘What are you then?’ said Susanne.

Jon took off his sunglasses and smiled at her. She could smell coffee on his breath. His teeth were perfect. ‘Canadian’, he said.

‘Oh well, I’m Irish’.

‘I’m looking for an Irish wife’, he said.

‘Sure you are’.

‘I’m very specific in what I want’, said Jon and then he smiled.

Susanne nodded towards the sea. ‘Why don’t you go back in there and cool off’.

‘Susanne isn’t a very Irish name’, Jon said. His shoulder glanced off hers as he turned to study her. ‘You look very Irish though’.

‘You don’t look Canadian’.

‘My mother was half-Chinese. My father was a small Dutchman from outside Amsterdam’. He breathed deep and Susanne saw his rib bones stand out. Jesus, she thought, am I about to be picked up by a thin tourist?

But then she looked at Jon’s feet again. They were milk coloured with blue veins and smooth, polished nails. He had moved his left one closer to her right and hers had a robust yellow hue with dry skin on its heel. She crabbed her toes into the ground to hide their dirt. ‘I’m hardly interested in being a wife’, she said aloud.

Jon shrugged. ‘No problem. If not you, then someone else’.

Susanne looked at him. ‘Who else?’

‘Could be anyone. Just has to be Irish’.

‘Why Irish?’

‘Romance’, he answered.

‘Oh for God’s sake’, said Susanne. ‘That’s only made up’.

‘You look like an Irish colleen’.

‘I look like shit’.

Jon looked at her straight shoulders and her flattened down

breasts underneath her tight blue swimsuit, and then her legs, her knees and her feet.

'You should protect your skin', he said. 'You'll burn'.

'I like getting hot', she replied.

Susanne shut her eyes against the beach glare and wished this Jon would vanish. Jesus ... an Irish wife. Every summer brought the idiot romantics, but usually she ignored them. Her two friends waved across at her and Susanne waved back. She heard Jon shift and noticed his shadow crawl and dip between the rocks. She could smell his fresh sweat and she closed her eyes. Her ears picked up his breathing and the garbled noises of the beach. She concentrated on her tight swimsuit and the pleasure it forced about her breasts while she moved her head in the direction of Jon's smell. She flexed her right foot and felt his left one slip beside hers.

It made her jerk, nearly made her come. The smooth, lukewarm skin of his foot across hers; the bridge of her foot locking into the arch of his, and then his lips just under her chin, then his teeth nipping a line to her collar bone.

Sand scratched between their feet. The weight of his foot dug hers deeper into the sand. She remembered her bedroom, the window open on hot days, the sunlight marking out the shadows of wardrobe, bed and desk; her sweat drying because of the tinge of cold that was always present. She shivered and he felt it.

She opened her eyes. His head was below her collarbone, his mouth above her breasts. His hair was toffee-colour with slick, fine curls at the base of his neck. She tried to straighten them with her fingers and they darkened in the sweat of his neck. She took only shallow breaths, all the more to feel the drag of pleasure. If he bit, then it would be perfect.

'Susanne?'

Susanne looked up. Her two friends stood dripping seawater and they hung onto their towels for something to do. 'Susanne?' they said again.

Susanne didn't bother answering, but closed her eyes, willing Jon to bite, which he did, which meant she married him that autumn.

On a hot morning in July nineteen-twenty-one, Alice and Martin arrived in Brighton. They sat watching the sea while others watched them.

People noticed Alice and Martin. She, for her beauty which she had always been used to; her turquoise eyes and remarkable face, pale and elongated, a living Modigliani with her chin length dark hair and dark pink mouth, and he, for his quivering head which Alice took care to ignore as best she could. She nibbled some chocolate and thought again what she meant to do. It would be managed, she decided.

Martin did not move beside her. He had hardly spoken to her, except once to remind her that the whole thing wasn't particularly necessary. He was no longer her lover, he was someone else's. He had such pride in him, as he told her. He was Thomas's now. Thomas let him breathe. Thomas demanded nothing.

But Martin was still beautiful to Alice. She had never forgotten that. In the beginning, his flinching head and deep animal eyes had been a challenge to her, one that had galvanised her idea of loving him.

'Thomas was right', she said aloud. 'A day away. Just perfect'.

She looked at Martin's face, at his scars, not all from the war, but from his own hand, and also from hers. They only heightened his beauty. She remembered the night he had demanded she slit his throat and, in fear, in fascination, she had held the knife at his jugular, his pleading furious eyes on her, his breath on her sweating fingers, and she had wondered then if he did die, how would it be afterwards? How would she be without him?

Life would return to normal as it always did whenever anyone left Alice. Thomas described it as her only ordinary flaw.

'You will people away', he said.

'Do I?' she sometimes wondered. Yet she rarely wished to understand since life was good despite the times alone, and usually another lover would slot in, filling those odd moments when she must have someone else; moments she could not describe aloud to anyone, but they were like blades in her gut.

Martin had regularly begged to die. He crawled beneath their bed to be away from her and she often left him there, returning later to find him at the kitchen table trying to write any story that came into his head. Sometimes he read it out and made her jealous. His words got into people. They got into her. People saw inside their minds what he wrote on the page.

I should have loved him more, thought Alice.

Thomas had been cruel when he agreed to her plan for the day. He laughed to begin with while he fixed his tie and then rubbed his teeth clean with one finger. He put on a show, demanding a shave from his new butler, moving about his *boudoir* where she had often been. The light caught on his collection of glass and gold figurines. He wondered aloud why she would request such a thing.

She shrugged and said she wanted to say goodbye. She said she deserved that much. 'I loved him once', she said.

'You were curious once', Thomas replied.

Alice had known Thomas ever since she had arrived in London. He helped her change her accent so it contained just the underlay of an Irish brogue. It kept her exotic, but approachable. He stood her in front of a mirror and ordered her to adopt Grecian poses. She had the correct lines, like a milk-coloured, untouchable boy and only her long hair and unlikely beautiful face - more beautiful without expression - meant she was a woman. Thomas taught Alice that the necessities of life depended on how much people wanted to be used by others.

Alice developed her natural capacity to use. She put it down to curiosity. Those who suffered fascinated her. She appreciated suffering. She liked to imagine the horror involved with such pain and how it could be so powerful as to leave its mark. She felt such a difference needed patronage and Alice became known for her odd choices. Even prostitutes from the street caught her eye. Thomas maintained it was 'dabbling', living life second-hand in order to spice up her published stories.

She tried other methods. She began stories in her own fashion, stories she thought she might remember from her home and childhood. Her grandfather had owned two horses that he had loved. Her mother loathed smelling of the farm and rarely ate. There had been brothers and sisters, but Alice had forgotten them. Too Irish to remember. Too noisy and too dirty.

Her father had loved Mass and admired the local priest's notions, one of which was that Alice had an intelligent face and should continue with her education. Alice continued. It meant her way out. She was sent to Dublin and lost her virginity after a night out at a local cheap opera. She adored clothes that said she was somebody. Clothes of deep colours: purple, blues, crimson, black jet beads and silk underwear.

Yet all this education never fit into what she wrote. It had no flow, Thomas informed her. So Alice wrote stories of the people she found, and most of them accepted her plunder since she paid well.

She became known. She was 'The Extraordinaire', capable of discovering people who became talking points in conversations, people who usually had a unique talent, and then drifted into being the crowd and sometimes discovered their own niche. Others were more strange and soon disappeared when Alice came to her senses, but all found their way into her stories.

Alice smiled out to the sea. A hot, busy day in Brighton had never been part of her imagined ending. In the beginning, she and Martin had done everything together. They had socialised with exciting friends and lived life on a comfortable edge. They spent a summer in Paris, without Thomas, and there for a brief six weeks Alice made love to a sculptor, while Martin attended an analyst.

That had failed when Alice discovered him staring into the mirror, his knuckles dug into his head and his whole body carved with that intense, dangerous effort which she had lusted after, now directed only at his reflection.

'You're forgetting me', she had accused.

Brighton promenade wearied Alice. It was crowded, too full of band music and children licking ices. She touched Martin's hand. It didn't move beneath her fingers.

'We should walk', she said and rose. She decided to remain silent until she knew exactly what to say. What was left now? What filled her? Neither her poetry nor her stories satisfied her anymore. Her editor had been very kind. He said all writers grew a chrysalis at times. They needed hibernation too, then poof! Crack! They emerged new and thrilling. He advised her to stop writing and experience more of life.

When Alice had first seen Martin, she had wanted him. He was a late arrival to Thomas's party and found a seat next to a naked, well-breasted young woman who hummed to music. She was very popular with everyone. She dangled her legs across Martin's lap and laughed at anyone's funny story. Alice didn't need to know her name. Girls like that had nothing in them, and if they had, it was buried deep under drugs and wine. A girl like that would only fill out two sentences in a story.

But Martin was different. It was nineteen-nineteen and he was a promising writer. He had suffered in the war and his face had deep bracket lines on each side of his mouth. His red hair was thick and shone as he bent every so often to kiss the girl's breasts.

Thomas laid his fingers on Alice's shoulder.

'They make a startling picture', he approved. 'A shivering head and singing breasts'.

'He might hear you, Thomas'.

'He's piss-poor and quite dirty. Like him?'

'Interesting', replied Alice.

'He loves being interesting', said Thomas. 'All new writers do. It's like a currency with them. Better than food. Certainly an improvement on sex!'

Thomas kissed Alice's cheek. 'My beautiful half-boy'.

She felt his smooth skin and inhaled hard on her cigarette. He kissed the skin behind her long earrings and said. 'Beware your curiosity, Alice'.

Alice ignored his smile and shook herself from his grasp. Thomas gave a low bow, then fixed his hand on some pretty acquaintance and was drawn away. Alice turned to see Martin watching her. He flipped the naked girl's legs from his lap, stood and also bowed. 'Alice Roe: The Extraordinaire'.

They danced together.

'I've read a little of your work', she lied.

He gave a wide, desperate smile and Alice saw he was missing two back teeth. 'And?' he demanded.

Alice admired that approach. Most new writers insisted on being coy. 'I like it all', she smiled.

He nodded. His lips were thin. A little spittle collected at one corner of his mouth. A side effect of the head shaking, she assumed. She pressed close against him.

'I have always wanted to write', he said. 'Always'.

'It's obvious'. She remarked.

'Ever since I can remember ... ever since things were real to me'.

His gaze juddered away from her, studying the room and those watching him dance with Alice. 'You're famous, Alice'.

'Thank you', she said.

He kissed her neck. She laughed and held her fingers beneath his chin. His head shook harder. 'Nothing stops it', he said.

She asked him about his home and he replied he had none really. A mother dead three years and a father still drunk in a Suffolk village. He had no one else. Later, in his iron bed with her back against the damp, papered wall, Alice read his work.

He wrote he could no longer love God. He wrote about the dirt men grasped as they died. He wrote his soul down on paper and Alice finally said. 'I think people want to forget the war'.

His shoulders were thin and pale against her own. She kissed his forehead and said. 'You will have to write about happier things as well'.

Martin's kisses trembled and his fingers liked to hurt, but Alice developed a tolerance for that. At night he whispered his nightmares into her throat. His sweat made her smell and she had sponge baths everyday. He wrote as she advised, but even then his soul crept into his stories, displaying a savage pain she could hardly bear. The pain she had seen in the prostitutes, in odd and various lovers, in her own forgotten parents, all of whose pain she had once filtered into her work, lived in Martin's.

'A writer', declared Thomas.

Thomas had christened the whole episode: 'Alice's Heathcliff Phase'. He threw parties in which Martin took centre stage as well as Thomas's attention.

'You'll use him', Alice accused.

'He'll survive it', Thomas replied.

Alice saw Thomas's smooth cream skin against Martin's patched face, her insides cracked and she realised she was losing something she had hardly known. By the kitchen table she re-read Martin's stories and realised how she had failed. She had nothing of his brilliance. She pressed her hand against her clothes-covered heart, then she ripped them until she felt her breast. Her heart beat. It was normal and yet inside it there was something she could not understand, an ... emptiness, and only Martin's stories reached inside.

And now finally as they walked along the pier, she decided to say something absolute and brave; something he could write into a story. Something no one could ever expect of her.

'Tell me to leave', she told Martin. 'Tell me to leave so I can'.

She stared into his silent, shattered face. She tried to follow his gaze, his eyes, and willed them to physically fill her, but it was useless.

He said goodbye first and left her there. She waited a long time before finding a café and sat sideways at a half-mirrored wall. She ordered chocolate ice-cream and ate steadily. Finally, she looked at her reflection. She lifted her chin to see herself more. She imagined her heart and wondered if it was as smashed as it could possibly be. Her heart's emptiness gnawed her. There was nothing to fill it now.

Perhaps it is a broken heart, she thought.

She smiled at her reflection and decided it suited her.

Two vampires cross the road, enter a café and order eggs. The shorter vampire has a tight, thin face with almost yellow eyes. His name is Robert and he is Welsh. He is one hundred years old and prefers French sixties clothes.

His companion, Francis, is taller and darker. He was originally thirty two years old some twenty years ago and had been an architect. His premature grey hair has a little black laced through it, and the last human thing he remembers is his wife calling to him.

While the two vampires await their eggs, they study the café's clientele, which is mainly young since the school day has just ended. Francis is not interested in them, but in the small, thin, blonde waitress who has taken their order. Robert also watches her. His face has stiffened as it always does when he sees prey. After some seconds he nods and nonchalantly wets his fingertips; trails sugar across them and then sucks each one clean.

Francis places the sugar dispenser out of reach, sits into his corner seat and lays his head back as if tired. He listens to the sounds around him. It is a habit and in the café's light and in the stretch of his body, he is aware of how normal he appears.

Robert, however, is anxious. He is disturbed by humans and only considers them as food. When he kills them, he hides their faces with his hand, shutting off their eyes and their mouths. Francis says it's because Robert must still remember how things had been, how things had once felt, but Francis is a romantic and believes in such things.

Robert likes the death he forces into humans. He likes how their skin tears under his teeth and how their attempts at screaming turn to nothing in his ears. He has stopped remembering anything of his life before, yet in the beginning, like Francis, he presumed he could not forget. He expected to remember how the smell of fresh bread filled a morning or how he always longed to be clean ... but he forgot it all.

Now he appreciates the distance between him and humans.

Their lives are alien, only their blood means anything. Robert once tried to explain it to Francis who did not listen, not because he was not interested, but because his hatred for Robert - although finally vague after all these years together - remained inside him still.

And Robert cannot explain. Not really, and not with any real care. Instead he accepts two things. Humans are food and Francis is beautiful - a vampire Robert believes he himself should have been - with a long, lazy naturalism in his body and rapid eyes that choose prey, in spite of the fact that blood is almost wasted on Francis. His hatred for Robert has seen to that.

Francis understands that blood means survival and he cannot consider his life without it, otherwise there is only starvation, a slow dessication of skin and bones. Since his soul is gone, he believes so might he be, and that is why he insists on remembering and coaxing the hate in his heart. It keeps him as himself.

Yet they have remained together. There is no answer for that and neither of them mentions it, and through the years they have developed a rhythm in their dead lives, culminating in one necessary ritual.

Every so often, they share a victim. They take turns to choose and kill. Robert is invariably quick; hand over face and teeth in neck. When he kills, he knows Francis is resentful. Francis likes to hear their voices, likes to see their faces. That is his romance and he has never lost it.

When Francis kills, he kills with an awe that Robert cannot stomach, for he knows what killing means to Francis. It means a few seconds of his vanished past, a few seconds for the memory of his wife.

Francis has opened his eyes and now watches the waitress approach their table. He can smell the fat-grease that has spattered her apron. Curls show from beneath her cap, and on each palm she balances their plates of eggs. She is nervous because of Francis's gaze as she fixes knives and forks on either side of each plate.

Francis smiles at her and she returns it. Her smile makes her look younger. 'Coffee's on its way', she tells them and retreats.

'You'll frighten her away', warns Robert.

'I won't', promises Francis.

Robert plunges his knife into his eggs. With one finger, he cleans up the yolk dribble and then licks it. His eyes fasten on Francis who cuts his eggs into strips before eating.

'Why not one of those school-kids?' demands Robert. 'You can pick one off easy. They don't always travel home in packs'.

Francis shrugs and does not need to answer. Robert knows he should be used to it all by now. When it is Francis's turn, a woman is always chosen.

Robert studies the waitress. What he can remember of women is very little. In his time as a human, they were as desperate as he. They littered the streets with their cries and perhaps he fucked some, but he soon forgot the sound and smell of them.

The waitress returns with coffee and smiles at Francis. She pours coffee into their cups and Robert looks at her neck while he avoids her face. Her neck is freckled, dainty and ageing. He sees where he would shove her throat back with the heel of his hand if she were his choice.

She talks about the weather to Francis and her right ankle bends sideways like a young girl, delighted and shy and not the tired woman she is. Robert looks at Francis's face and his stomach constricts when he sees that Francis's gaze on the woman is clear and has that strange beauty. Beneath his eyes, the skin is dark as if he could still have his own blood there. His smile is always as he makes it, inviting, warm and human-like. He is pointing at her apron.

'Oh, Jesus ... this', she flaps her apron out from her dress. 'The cook's sick and I got roped in'.

Francis sips his coffee and then slots his long hands into each other over his cup and smiles still.

'I cooked your eggs', she nods at their plates.

'We know', snaps Robert.

Francis ignores him and examines the waitress's face. She has pale skin with light freckles. Her eyes are light brown, narrow and small. Nothing like his wife. Nothing like her face which still comes to him, even if at times he has to claw its memory back. And her smell had been nothing like grease. It had been ... Here, he fails to remember, because her exact smell left him long ago, and the smells of the women he kills now are only approximations.

Some women are clean. Others are stale with perfume, while others smell of sweat or merely of themselves. Those are the ones he prefers. He wants to remember that his wife smelt like herself when he had left her that morning, and also that she had smiled at him, and if there had been a kiss, he can imagine it.

He says something that never fails. 'You have a beautiful smile'.

The waitress is pleased. She curls her notepad in her palm and then releases it. 'Would you like something else?' she asks.

'What's your name?'

'Lillian'.

Francis smiles. 'Old-fashioned'.

'My grandmother's. She made my parents' life hell until they gave it to me. I wasn't baptised with it. That's a different name. But I was given "Lillian". My grandmother made sure of that'.

Lillian holds her pencil above her notepad. 'Anything else?'

'More coffee', Francis says.

She adds coffee to his cup and then swings the coffee-pot towards Robert who stands up fast and silent. His yellow eyes slit at her and she almost yelps with fear. She steps back and then gathers up a smile. 'Sorry. I'm in your way', she says.

Robert looks at Francis. 'I'll be outside', and leaves.

Lillian watches him go. 'Is he okay?'

'He just wants some cold air', explains Francis and indicates she should sit. Lillian checks that none of the other staff are watching and sits in Robert's place.

Francis leans in towards her and she still seems shy. 'Lillian'.

'Yes?'

'How is it that you are here?'

He calculates that she will think this an unusual start, and he has picked its deliberate phrasing because she has a smell about her now, not the grease, since her apron is hidden under the table, but a sullen odour of heavy perfume on her blouse. Francis has learned that women who want more in life use perfumes of that kind.

Kitchen sweat has made her face gleam and about her are the sounds of the diner. Clacking cutlery, the drift and soar of voices, eating and the swing of the entrance door all collect about her and she becomes real to him, in all her grease-sweat glory and girlish smile.

'It's just a job', she replies. She also leans forward and uses one finger to pull a curl from above her ear. 'It's a stop-gap. I have plans'. She then glances up and through the window she sees Robert standing on the path outside, his back to the café.

'Is he okay?'

Francis calls her attention back. 'What plans?'

'Oh, you know. Get out of here. Find a new life. Usual ones'.

'Specifically', he says, and, at her frown, 'I mean exactly what sort of plans? How do you plan to live a new life?'

Lillian bites her lip and lowers her voice. 'I plan to be an archaeologist'.

Francis expects this to be a lie. In a greasy-spoon café, in a dump of a town like this, to want to be an archaeologist is ridiculous.

'It's a good plan', Francis says.

She nods. 'Always loved history and old things. Used to dig up the back garden when I was small. Found loads of crap'.

Her eyes glisten and inside Francis's cold skin and behind his bones, he is sure something stirs. 'When do you finish work, Lillian?'

Lillian pinches her fingers as she considers. 'In half an hour'.

He nods. 'We can meet outside'.

She nods back. 'Yeah. Sure. Yeah. That's fine'.

'An archaeologist', he compliments her.

She slips out of her seat and smoothes her apron across her stomach. Someone yells her name and she flicks a smile at Francis before returning to work.

Francis continues to drink his coffee. He does not need to glance at the window to know that Robert is still standing outside, nursing his suffering and his hunger. Francis knows that Robert will always wait, will continue with the ritual because Francis desires his revenge this way; because Francis's own hate will not allow him to continue his dead life alone, and because until the day Robert had made Francis a vampire, Robert had always been lonely.

It had happened on a hot Saturday afternoon and perhaps he had been working overtime or maybe he had been shopping, but Francis had rung his wife. He listened to her voice until there was a sudden pain and a pull on his blood as if the whole of him was being dragged away. Robert had him.

From that moment on, Francis has fed on two things; blood and his frustrated hate for Robert. This hate has made his heart live inside him. He kills people desperate to be a part of them, whole and real again, but that has never happened, and there is only Robert with his skinny face, his accent and his loneliness so powerful that it is like a smell from which Francis cannot escape.

Yet somehow he plucked forward into his mind the memories Robert wished he would forget. A wife and her voice. How she must have been to him. How beautiful. How loving.

Francis leaves a tip beside his cup and makes his way over to pay at the cash register where another waitress, spotty and disinterested, takes his money. Lillian catches his eye and he nods at her. She watches him exit the café and join Robert. They talk for a few seconds and then Francis is left alone.

When Lillian finishes work, she finds Francis waiting by a car. She gives him an easy smile and they walk out to a pub.

'Where's your friend?' she asks.

'Found something to do', Francis replies.

Inside, the pub is empty except for the landlady who stands up from a seat behind the bar and greets them.

'Monday night', says Lillian.

She sits and from her dress pocket she takes a packet of cigarettes, but Francis refuses her offer, and, while she lights one up, he gives their order to the landlady.

Lillian smokes and watches Francis. She flicks ash onto the floor. 'You seem nice', she tells him. She inhales, looks down and then up. 'I meet men'.

'Often?'

'Sometimes'.

Francis smiles. There is a cough in the darkness beyond their alcove and Lillian swivels to see the landlady placing their drinks on the bar's counter. Francis collects them.

'I like your hands', Lillian says, then drinks with determined gulps.

'Really?' Francis turns his right hand palm upwards as Lillian touches it.

'Hmm. They're thin. Long. Very artistic'.

Francis drinks and listens. He likes to talk with the women he has decided to kill, and he prefers to disregard their normal expectation of a quick fuck after a session of drinks. Instead he studies their faces and tries to remember his wife's.

Sometimes these women spoke of sadness, of lives ruined by death and mistakes, or of children, or of how their jobs hardly mattered and were only stop-gaps.

In each conversation, Francis understands that he is seeing lives he can never possess, only destroy, and because of this he never thinks beyond his victim's death or the consequences for whatever lives they leave behind.

He is like Robert in this respect. When the blood is drunk and the body left, there is only the fact that their small ritual has ended until the next time, and they return to their usual hunt.

'You're an artist', Lillian says.

'Yes', lies Francis.

'What kind?'

'Sculpture'.

'I can tell'.

She smiles and inside Francis there is a mixture of hunger for her blood and hunger for what her smile may mean. She takes his hand and her nails trace the veins on its back.

'I love beautiful hands. You know, people warn you about faces, never about hands ... and what they can do'. She drops his hand and raises her empty glass. 'I'd like another. Hey!' She yells at the landlady. 'More for each of us'.

'You're a fast drunk', remarks Francis.

'I need to be. No ... let her bring them. Stay with me'. Lillian smiles and taps her fingers on the table. 'They warn you about everything else. All the dangerous stuff like this ...' she jerks her head towards the drinks the landlady places on the table. Francis pays, but the landlady remains where she is, first glancing at the drinking Lillian and then addressing Francis. 'I'll be busy out the back for a while. If you want anything else, you'll have to come to the bar and shout'.

She returns to the bar and puts Francis's money in the till. She then disappears into the back.

'I drink too much, I know', Lillian confesses. 'All because I love beautiful hands like yours'. She pauses. 'But you couldn't be bothered with my story, could you? You've got something else on your mind'.

'Just talk', says Francis.

'I'm tired', she says and does not notice Robert move out from the darkness. Francis glances at the bar. Empty. Robert is trembling from hunger, but waits. Francis whispers something and Lillian puts down her glass.

'Sorry?' she asks.

Francis whispers again and Lillian frowns. He leans forward so that her face is near his, he is near to her eyes that shine now, and abruptly his wife is as beautiful as he remembers, and he says her name.

Lillian makes a face. 'That's not my name. "Anna" is not my name'. She peers at his face. 'You're staring'.

Robert coughs behind and nods a greeting when Lillian turns and then scowls at him. To Francis she says. 'He's come back.

Make him leave'.

'He doesn't hear you', Robert says.

'Of course he hears me. He's looking at me, isn't he?'

Robert steps close. He draws his hands up to touch the curls that lie above Lillian's ears.

'Francis doesn't see you, Lillian'.

She half-laughs and clicks her fingers in Francis's face. There's no reaction.

'For God's sake', she mutters. 'Not very polite'.

'No', says Robert.

'Is it epilepsy?' she asks.

'Kind of'. Robert uses one hand to stroke the jagged middle split in Lillian's hair and he hears the effect on her breath.

'Kiss him', he orders.

Lillian presses her face forwards and for a galvanised few seconds, Robert looks and sees what has always terrified him - all Francis's worn beauty almost alive.

Pain opens up inside him and to defeat it, he reaches out his other hand and swipes the glasses out of Francis's way.

'Jesus', cries Lillian.

She tries to move, but Robert's grip prevents her. She tries to scream, but Francis lunges. His teeth gouge her neck, while her last breath is smothered by Robert's hand.

Together they take her outside and find a hiding place where Robert drinks his fill and, when he is finished, they fold the body into a nearby rubbish bin. They say nothing to each other. Francis never speaks of what he remembers, and Robert has learned not to ask. They remain silent as Robert drives their car onto the road. His fingers are nearly warm on the steering wheel, but will slowly cool as Lillian's blood finally becomes part of him.

He glances at Francis's face, then concentrates on his driving.

Never could remember when I started hating my younger sister, but it had been in me a long time. It wasn't even the day when she sashayed up to me and said. - You know, the village boys screw their sisters?

I choked on my beer and almost fell off the veranda. My friend David nearly pissed himself laughing.

- Fuck, he crowed. - Fuck your sister, man.

I punched him and his can of beer spun into the air as he crumpled to his knees. I grabbed his head and yelled into his face what kind of sick bastard says that shit?

- Jesus ... Jesus ... Theo, said David, and held his hands up in surrender. - It's a joke. It's only fun.

I dropped him and turned to look at Marianne, who said it's the truth.

- Screw you, Marianne.

- Theo, man, your sister knows what's what.

- Yeah, Theo. I know what's what.

I hated the way Marianne stood as if she were far older than seventeen. She stood like a mini-whore in shorts with one leg standing sideways, so David could see the whole inner thigh.

- Wear some goddamn clothes, I said.

- Make me.

I leaned back against the veranda pillar with another beer in my hand and said, - Get lost, little girl. Big boys want to talk. I burped and David burped back. Marianne was disgusted and flounced off. David reached for another beer and I handed it to him.

- Sorry, I said.

- No problem, he said.

- Shit my sister says pisses me off, I explained.

- Yeah. David drank and then said - But she's right, you know. All those weasels fuck their sisters. It's bred into them. Ever look at their kids? Eyes in the wrong places and shit. All fucking deformed. Hitler had the right idea about shit like that. Just get rid of what you don't need. Clean the place up.

- Sure, I said.

- Yeah you know what I'm talking about. They aren't like us. They'll never be us. That guy executed last week ...? Had his picture taken with Commies from overseas ...?

- Yeah what about him?

- Fucked his sister. David gargled loud before he gulped his drink.

- Bullshit, I said.

- No. It's documented. Signed the admission just before they hung the prick.

- Sure.

- I saw it.

- The hanging or the admission?

- He couldn't even write, continued David. Signed some mark. I'm going to get a copy and hang it up. Look cool on my wall.

- Did you see the hanging? I said.

David looked over my shoulder and I turned. There was no one there. - Just making sure, David said and punched my arm so I'd look at him. - Fucking awful mess.

- Yeah?

- They always try to stay alive. David mimed the face of a hanged man. - Piss and shit come running out. David opened another can. - Ever want to draw one?

- No.

- I'd say it'd be cool. Be a bit different to what you do.

I reached for the last can and pulled its tab. I sat back up on the veranda's wall and felt the hot sun on my feet. I wanted to forget where I was. I wanted the small crowd of people at the other end of the veranda to disappear. I wanted it to be night. A thick, soft night that held the whole day's sweat inside its dark gut. Those nights made me invincible. I could imagine anything those nights. I focussed my eyes on some new plant Mom had wound about the pillar. Dark green, no flower. I could paint that, I told myself. Mom made sure things looked good. Things always had to look good.

- I like what I do, I said.

- Yeah, well what the fuck do I know? I'm the philistine who prefers cars. You paint the pictures of pretty, pretty flowers and I drive the cars. Seriously, ever think of doing different pictures?

David used his smile full-force and my skin went cold. Outside I was calm. I even raised my eyebrows and spat hard against the dark green plant on the pillar.

I shrugged. - No interest, I said. - I'm a fucking botanist, or I will be when I graduate. I nodded at the plant. - That sort of thing. That gets me juiced.

David leaned against the wall, then leaned his head further back to catch the sun. He screwed his eyes against it and said. - Watching somebody die gets me juiced.

He wanted my reaction, and the sick thing is that David looked like his mother when he smiled. His mother had been cool. Long and toffee-colour tanned. I painted her many times, and at nights I'd hold my dick in my hand and imagine loving her. She was sweet. I could have taken care of her. I could have said to her ... yeah, all this shit gets to me too. All the fear and keeping quiet. Those fucking games we play. I could have told her that I was different and that we were two of a kind. I think she would have liked to have known there was somebody like her who knew - who just knew - that the things that happened on the streets or in the interrogation cells, opening your office door and finding the secret police instead of your secretary, all these things weren't supposed to be normal.

Instead she got into her car and gassed herself. I even drew that. Like going to sleep, I told myself. I pulled up the floorboards in my room and put that painting on top of the others. At night and in bed I stare at the rug that covers the exact spot, but I never manage to cry. I always felt she was still too real. I could still hold my dick and imagine her skin against my arms and the sweat between her breasts. Fucks me up to look at David now.

David was still smiling. I was cool. I scanned the empty beer cans.

- I need to piss and we need more beer.

I walked back in through the kitchen. Joseph the cook was scraping out the insides of two rabbits into a bowl. Mom must have told him to cook extra food.

- Hey Joseph, I said. - Being a bit prissy about the gutting, aren't you? Why use a knife? Didn't you learn how real men do it? Here. I'll demonstrate. I swung one up from the table and bent its fore and hind legs.

- You need to employ the catapult technique, I said and let fly. The guts slapped against the opposite wall, stuck for some seconds, then dropped to the floor. Joseph flicked his finger against his lips.

- Learned it in a book, I said. I dropped the rabbit back on the table and picked up a potato and onion. Joseph continued using the knife on the rabbit I had gutted for him.

- Hey Joseph, I said. - Maybe I should paint you one day.

Joseph had a small brown head and a thin moustache and his face was pock-marked with open pores. When I was younger I imagined he had worms with black eyes living there watching everything I did. I knew that's exactly how I would paint him. I saw it in my head. I saw the fucking worms turning so that their eyes could see me.

Joseph ignored me, picked up the bowl and tipped his rabbit's guts into the pedal bin. He took a wet cloth and wiped at my rabbit's gut-traces on the wall, and I remembered I had to piss, so I headed for the bathroom.

I liked the bathroom too. It helped me think. I had ideas in this bathroom. Crazy shit came into my head sometimes. Made my fingers itch to get the pictures down. Pictures crept into my head as if they crept into a church. I could see how things should be. I could see that if things were different, then I could walk out of my parents' house, walk down to the village, buy a drink, screw a girl if I wanted and make it home alive. Or I could imagine I was an artist who drew what he saw and could expect to survive.

A knock on the bathroom door, and I opened it. It was Marianne with a bottle of vodka and David behind her.

- Thought we could have these in your room, said Marianne. - We won't be missed. They're too busy getting drunk and David's dad is crying.

David shrugged and led the way to my bedroom. All three of us sat on my bed and drank from the vodka bottle. David watched Marianne's thighs, while I watched him.

- You're gonna miss her, I said.

- Who?

- Your mother, you prick.

- Sure I'll miss her. Sure. She was good. He made a face at Marianne who giggled. - Kept me clean. Tried to make me good. Just like any other mother.

- Our mother is a neurotic, said Marianne.

- Shut up, I told her.

David looked around my room, at the paintings on my walls. - Thought you said you were only interested in plants. I see a shit load of other things here as well. Is that you Marianne? Fuck ... how old are you in that?

- Eleven, I said.

- I'm telling you man, said David. - You've a gift.

David was right. I had a gift. His mother saw it straight away during one of those coffee mornings Mom had organised. I was home for the weekend and I stank from a basketball game. Mom tried to steer me away, but David's mom had seen me. She came up close so I could smell her ... came up very close so I could touch her.

- I was in your room, she said. - I got lost after visiting the bathroom and there was a paintbrush in the hallway near your door. I got curious, knocked on the door and pushed it in. She smiled. - My, have you got talent.

- Theo is going to be a botanist, said my mother.

David's mother nodded her head. - I like what you paint.

I shrugged. - It's a hobby. Sometimes I do commissions though. Guys want their girlfriends drawn ... you know.

- David hasn't any talent, said his mother. - He's just like his father. He prefers to crush things. She lifted her coffee cup to her lips and smiled over the rim at me. Her arms were gleaming brown and she wore a dark red dress tied at her waist. She didn't look old. She looked beautiful. She looked the way she did when I first painted her.

- Your mother was beautiful, I said aloud.

- She was a fool, David said.

Marianne raised her eyebrows at me and clamped her lips round the vodka bottle.

- Watch it, I told her.

She slurped the drink back, handed the bottle over to David and licked up any dribbles on her mouth. David leaned over and kissed her. Marianne squealed and play-slapped his face away, but she didn't fight back when he pulled at her feet, so her whole body faced him.

- She wasn't a fool, I said.

Marianne looked at me. - What did you say?

- David's mother wasn't a fool, I said. - And David knows it.

- She's dead now, Marianne said.

David leaned his face down so he could kiss her toes. She squealed again and bounced on the bed. The vodka bottle fell sideways and spilled on my jeans. I picked it up, gulped from it, then put it on the windowsill.

Marianne was still squealing.

- Shut up, I told her.

She stuck out her tongue. I reached up for the bottle and threw it at her face. It hit her nose and she held up her hands as blood spurted out into them.

David freaked. He screamed and scrambled off the bed. He stood in the middle of the room, sprayed with Marianne's blood, with his mouth opening and closing in shock.

There was a knock at the door and, when no one entered, I knew it was a servant. - Come in, I ordered.

Joseph came in. His face didn't change when he saw the blood on David and Marianne. He moved further into the room, level with David. Marianne's nose was still bubbling blood into her hands and she was still squealing like a little stuck pig. Joseph nodded at David and said. - Your father wants you, Mister David.

Maybe the blood frightened David. Maybe there are lots of reasons why David did what he did. Marianne now says it was grief. Maybe it was because Joseph smiled a minute smile and David saw it.

He punched Joseph's face so hard it snapped back, and there was the clear and inevitable sound of his neck cracking. He crumpled down, his legs splayed under his body and he sat, broken and dead in the middle of the room.

Not one of us moved.

- Is he dead? said David.

Marianne wiped at her face with my bed sheet. She turned to me and snarled. - Look at what you've done!

- I didn't kill him, I said.

She looked at Joseph's body. - I don't mean him. She pointed at her nose. - I mean my 'dose'!'

I laughed. I screwed my body up and I laughed. I laughed because my body was shaking. I laughed because Marianne's snivelling was too strong and I had to drown it out. I laughed because Marianne couldn't see what was in front of her nose. I heard David laughing as well and then he said. - You can draw that, can't you?

I stopped laughing and looked at Joseph. His eyes were staring at the opposite wall. He was sitting in almost the same place as David's mother once sat in a chair, smiling for me. I knew what I was seeing when I looked at Joseph, but I didn't want it to be real, so I closed my eyes.

- He asked for it, David said.

I kept my eyes closed.